PROPHETIC MENTORING

With
FOUNDATIONS FOR
SPIRITUAL MATURITY

Teachers Manual

Kenneth Peters Jr.

But Moses said to him, "Are you jealous for my sake?
Would that all the LORD'S people were prophets, that the LORD would put His
Spirit on them!"

Numbers 11:29

CONTENTS

DEDICATION AND ACKNOWLEDGMENTS

This book is dedicated to the memory of my late husband, Kenneth Peters, and Bishop Bill Hamon for their many years and sacrifices for the body of Christ.

Thank you to my husband for his many years of sacrifice, training, and equipping the church. Under the permission of Bishop Bill Hamon, Ken wrote the Advanced Prophetic Training Manual and Foundations for Spiritual Maturity (which includes the 10 M's coined by Bishop Hamon), all of which are included in this manual. Ken believed that we could be trained in the prophetic, but if a leader's life and character were out of order, it would be unfruitful. Ken used these manuals for over 3 decades of training leaders for the work of ministry.

Thank you to Bishop Bill Hamon for his many years of service and training in the prophetic. His influence in our lives motivated the thousands of individuals who received this training over the last three decades in our lives.

Tonja Peters

WHY A PROPHETIC TRAINING CLASS?

Numbers 11:23-29

Joel 2:28-29

1 Corinthians 12:1-11

Verse 11 "will" Greek: *boulomahee* #1014 & 2309

To will, be willing, intends, desires, inclined to, to wish

This word used is a completely different expression than #2309 *theleo*, which denotes an objective consideration, choose, choice or prefer.

1 Corinthians 14:1-40

Verse 3   edification, exhortation, comfort, (not limited to one individual)

Verse 5   rather that you prophesied, than all speak with tongues, for he is greater!

Verse 12   seek to excel to edify the church through prophecy, only prophecy!

Verse 24   but if *all* prophesy…he is convinced of *all*…he is judged of *all*

Verse 31   you *all* may prophesy, one by one that *all* may learn, *all* may be comforted!

1 Thessalonians 5:11-22

Despise not #1848 *exoutheneo*

Contempt, esteem lightly, set at naught, to make utterly nothing of, disdain

(1 Corinthians 14:39-40 KJV) *Wherefore, brethren, **covet** to prophesy, and forbid not to speak with tongues. {40} Let all things be done decently and in order.*

Covet #2206 *zeloo:* envy, jealous over, zealously affected, sanctified lust.

1

EXPOSING FEAR AND UNWORTHINESS

A. Fear and Unworthiness ---- Two biggest obstacles to overcome

   1. *2 TIMOTHY 1:6-7*   We are called to make _changes_ into others _lives_.

   2. Why do we fight change?

      a. Prophet can _impart_ to the _believer_.

      b. Don't miss _impartation_ because of someone's _personality_. It is the _anointing_ that gets _imparted_.

   3. Remember God will offend our _minds_ to _reveal_ our _hearts_.

   4. Fear is _sin_. *1 Timothy 4:14*   *Hebrews 2:3-4*

      Neglect is the result of fear and a lack of understanding

B. *COLOSSIANS 1:10*

   1. God has anointed us the same as _Jesus_.   *ROMANS 1:4*

   2. Jesus was made _perfect_ through _suffering_ we are _too_.

   3. When your desire to _bless_ others exceeds the fear of _missing_ it or of making a _mistake_, then you can _minister_ the way Jesus did.

   4. Anytime you say, "I can't," you _curse_ yourself and _God_.

C. *Prayer and Deliverance Time*

   Fear, unworthiness, intimidation and inadequacy

APPLICATION: ONE ON ONE PRAYING.

LEVEL I THE DEEPER FLOW

ENTERING THE DEEPER FLOW

God wants to open our <u>ears</u> and open our <u>mouths</u>.

1. Open #6605 –*pathach*: To open wide, to loosen, to plow, to break forth, to draw out, let go free, to unstop, to ungird, to vent.
2. We need to pray likc David: (Psalm 51:15) "O Lord, open thou my <u>lips;</u> and my <u>mouth</u> shall shew forth thy <u>praise</u>.
3. Why? Because we are living in the day that Isaiah and Joel prophesied!

ISAIAH 41:18   ***"I WILL OPEN UP RIVERS IN THE HIGH PLACES, AND FOUNTAINS IN THE MIDST OF THE VALLEYS: I WILL MAKE THE WILDERNESS A POOL OF WATER, AND THE DRY LAND SPRINGS OF WATER."***

JOEL 3:18   ***"AND IT SHALL COME TO PASS IN THAT DAY, THAT THE MOUNTAINS SHALL DROP DOWN NEW WINE, AND THE HILLS SHALL FLOW LIKE MILK AND ALL THE RIVERS OF JUDAH SHALL FLOW WITH WATERS, AND A FOUNTAIN SHALL COME FORTH FROM THE HOUSE OF THE LORD AND SHALL WATER THE VALLEY OF SHITTIM."***

A. Where can we expect the <u>flow</u>? In the Valley of Shittim!! Shittim was another name for Acacia. The Valley of Shittim was the place where Joshua commanded the people to prepare to go into the promise land. It was a valley that had thousands of Acacia trees. Acacia wood represented humanity; the Ark of the Covenant was constructed of Acacia wood—the dwelling place of God: humanity. God says that in the day of the Joshua Generation, He will bring us into the Valley of the Acacias and in this Valley, we can expect new wine, new milk and a flow of God's water His prophetic Word.

B. Joshua was commanded to take the children of Israel to a land flowing with milk and honey. God wants to take us to a new position where we find the promised flow of New Testament honey the Word of the Lord. (Revelation 10:9 and Ezekiel 3:1-4)

INGREDIENTS TO THE DEEPER FLOW

A. <u>Faith</u> - Romans 12:6
B. Confidence: <u>Confidence</u> in His <u>calling</u> and His <u>commissioning</u>. Proverbs 14:26
C. <u>Obedience</u>: Obeying the <u>voice</u> of the Holy Spirit; to step out when the <u>opportunity</u> arises. 1 Samuel 15:22
D. Boldness: Not based on <u>personality</u>, vocabulary, or <u>education</u>. Proverbs 28:1
E. Willingness to take <u>risks</u>: "Yes, there are giants in the land." 1 Samuel 17:29-51
F. <u>Determination</u>: based upon <u>God</u>-given <u>vision</u>. Proverbs 10:4
G. Practice: <u>Prophesy</u> to the wind. Hebrews 5:14
H. Mentoring/Association: Elijah- <u>Elisha</u> 2 Kings 2:1-14

PROPHETIC APPLICATION: Writing the thoughts of the Lord.

- This can be through a thought, impression, or scripture:

_____

_____

_____

_____

_____

_____

_____

_____

_____

_____

_____

_____

_____

_____

_____

_____

_____

KEYS TO THE DEEPER FLOW

A. Realize that your <u>confidence</u> in God will begin to exceed <u>your</u> confidence in having to <u>see</u>, hear, or <u>feel</u> something before you <u>prophesy</u>. Like a <u>river</u>, if you <u>open</u> the dam <u>water</u> will come <u>out</u>.

B. Realize there are different <u>levels</u> of flowing:

Water can be found in:

1. <u>Springs</u> - clear, cool, but usually <u>hidden</u>.

2. <u>Streams</u> – no <u>flow</u> or <u>force</u>.

3. Lazy flowing <u>rivers</u>: lots of <u>water</u> but it meanders all over the <u>place</u>.

4. White-water <u>rapids</u>: like a rafter, you <u>learn</u> to go with the <u>flow</u> and avoid the <u>danger</u> areas.

C. Realize that there are <u>seasons</u> of flowing: <u>Rivers</u> usually peak in the spring. You will go through <u>times</u> and <u>seasons</u> when you feel dry... that's when you must learn to <u>dig</u> deeper for the <u>underground</u> river.

1. *Ezekiel 43:2*   Ezekiel saw the Glory of God coming from the east gate... "His <u>voice</u> was like the roar of rushing <u>waters</u>."

2. The desire to bless others must exceed the fear of mistakes or missing it.

Humanity vs. Pride.

3. **Ezekiel 47:6-12** There is a <u>river</u> from the <u>temple</u> that <u>flows</u> continually.

4. There is a time for the temple to be <u>filled,</u> but there is also a time when the temple doors open and <u>water</u> is allowed to <u>flow</u> out. The New Apostolic temple based upon God's pattern is <u>designed</u> to allow the <u>flow</u> of God's <u>rushing</u>, roaring <u>water</u> out!

D. Realize there is a <u>diversity</u> of flows:

We must make provision for <u>different</u> administrations of the same <u>manifestation</u>. Just as God can and does heal many ways, so can He minister prophetically many different ways.

E. Realize that what God considers <u>accurate</u> and what others consider <u>accurate</u> can be quite <u>different</u>. Accuracy must be judged on <u>fruit</u>.

F. Realize you must <u>yield</u> to Holy Spirit's <u>stretching</u>: New levels for new devils.

Example: When prophesying over people, don't ask them their names and see if the Lord will give you a name while you are ministering to them.

HINDRANCES TO THE FLOW

A. Fear of Man
B. Theology
C. Fear of not articulating correctly
D. Fear due to other's "horror stories"
E. Division of soul and spirit
   1. Unforgiveness
   2. Bitterness
   3. Resentment

PROPHETIC ACTIVATION: Believe for a Word of Knowledge: (It's ok to ask God questions)

Word of Knowledge: This serves as a true *faith builder* for the person receiving the prophetic word as precise details about their life are revealed through someone that doesn't have prior knowledge about them.

From the Strong's Concordance: G1108 gnosis, gno'-sis From G1097; knowing (the act), by implication) knowledge: - knowledge, science.

Definition:

- Supernatural revelation given by the Holy Spirit to a believer about specific facts in the mind of God for another. These facts are accurate and may give information about a person's past, present, or future.
- It is an instant knowledge from the Lord that the recipient has no way of knowing except that God reveals it.

_____
_____
_____
_____
_____
_____
_____
_____
_____
_____
_____
_____
_____
_____
_____

LEVEL II PRINCIPLES

The deeper flow, more accurate revelation, stronger anointing, prophetic credibility, increased fulfillment, and signs and wonders: these are all desires deep within the heart of every prophetic son or daughter of God.

I SAMUEL 3:1-20

This passage tells us that Samuel grew, and the Lord was with him. He did not let any of his words fall to the ground, and all Israel knew that Samuel had been established as a prophet of the Lord.

Three times the scriptures declare Samuel grew on two of those occasions he was said to be a child. However, on the last occasion Samuel was a man.

1. Grow

2. The Lord was with him

3. Guarded his words

WHAT WILL KEEP OUR WORDS FROM FALLING TO THE GROUND?

A. *Relationship: Psalm 25:14*

1.   The _secret_ of the Lord is with them who _fear_ Him.

2.   _Reverence_ only comes through _intimacy_.

   How intimate are you with the Lord? Do you press into knowing Him?

3.   Are you _searching_ for Him with all your _heart?_

4.   Do you _seek_ look for the Lord? (hide-n-seek) Jeremiah *29:11-14*

B. *Consecration: 1 Thessalonians 4:3*

   1.   This is the _will_ of God: our _sanctification_.

       That you possess your own _vessel_ in sanctification and _honor_.

   2.   Be ye _separate_, touch not the _unclean_ thing.

   3.   *Titus 2:11-14* _Consecration_ = _good_ _works_.

       Be zealous of good works

   4.   *Ephesians 2:10* says, We are His workmanship created in Christ Jesus for _good_ _works_, which God predestined that we should walk in them.

C. *The Word   2 Timothy 3:16-17*

   1.   The Word of God is our _lamp_ and light, our _illumination_.

       Revelation only comes as a _flow_ to the prophet who is in God's _Word_.

   2.   The New Testament _prophet_ can only _prophesy_ that which is _revealed_ truth from the _Word_ of _God_.

   3.   You must _fill_ your _well_ with God's _Word_ which bring _life_.

D. *Faith   Romans 12:6*

   1.   Having then gifts _differing_ according to the grace that is given to us, let us use them; let us _prophesy_ according to the proportion of our _faith_.

   2.   Is our _level_ of _faith_ limited? NO!

   3.   *Hebrews 11:6* *"Without _faith_ it is impossible to please Him..."*

       faith = _seeking_ _Him_

   4.   *Hebrews 11:1*   _Faith_ is the _evidence_ of things not seen = _revelation_

   5.   *Romans 10 :17*   _Faith_ comes by _hearing_ ...listening

   6.   *Jude 20*   _Build_ your faith by _praying_ in the Holy Ghost.

   7.   *James 2:26*   Faith without _works_ is dead, Faith grows by _works_.

E. *Use of Gift   Mark 4:24 (NKJV)*

   1.   Take heed what you _hear_ , with the same _measure_ you _use_ , is the same measure you will _receive_ .

       Use Little = Receive Little   Use Much = Receive Much

   2.   *1 Peter 4:10*   As you have <u>received</u> a gift even so <u>minister</u> it to one another as good <u>stewards</u>. If you don't use your gift, what kind of stewards are we?

   3.   Parable of the talents

   4.   *Hebrews 5:14*   Reason of use

F. *Prayer / Intercession Watchman   Ezekiel 3:10, 17, 25-27*

  Rules of the Prophets

   1.   God's words must _first_ go to our _hearts,_ then our _ears_ . Our _ears_ have no compassion and no _emotions_ to stir us to _pray,_ to _intercede_ , and to stand in the gap. But our _hearts_ do, therefore God first _speaks_ to our heart!

   2.   God has _made_ thee a _watchman._ Watchmen love the inhabitants of the _city,_ this is why they don't _sleep_ on the job. _Love_ proves out their _diligence._

      Jesus said watch and pray. The two go hand in hand.

      A prophet who doesn't pray prior to ministry is a clanging gong...

      We are Priests who enter the Holy Place on behalf of God's people!

            What an honor God has bestowed upon us!

      Prophets are not to be _reprovers_ . Let God make your _tongue_ cling to the roof of your _mouth_ , then when He _speaks_ , let Him _loose_ your tongue.

G. *Anointing / Wisdom & Understanding   1 John 2:27*

   1.   We have an _anointing_ that _abides_ and <u>lives</u> in <u>us</u> from Christ. This _unction_ of the Holy One will _teach_ us if we _allow_ it to. However this takes _time_ .

           Time & Relationship = Trust = Confidence

   2.   Confidence is something gained through _time._ The <u>anointing</u> brings confidence!

   3.   The _anointing_ is God's seal of ordination. It is the anointing that destroys the <u>yoke.</u>

     a.   Strive for God's anointing on your life to be _manifested._

b. God's anointing comes as a <u>still</u> small <u>voice</u>, not in fanfare and side shows.

c. Purity, <u>holiness</u>, and <u>consecration</u> bring <u>release</u> to the anointing.

d. Your <u>word</u> can be right, but <u>without</u> the anointing it is void of <u>power</u> to accomplish God's <u>desired</u> purposes.

4. *Isaiah 55...*

"The anointing is the tangible authority of the believer, the authorization from heaven upon a believer to do the work of God—the power that causes the accomplishment of the purposes of God."

PROPHETIC PROTOCOL

A. The Word of the _Lord_ in the mouth of the _untrained_ brings _destruction_ and death rather than _healing_ and _life_.

B. Fineness and excellence come first through _watching_.

C. Always, _always_, always speak the _word_ of the Lord in the _Spirit_ of the Lord.
    1. Gentleness
    2. Kindness
    3. Goodness
    4. Self-control
    5. Peace

    The Word of the Lord brings life, it is the _well-spring_ of life.

D. At this _juncture_ avoid words of _strong_ correction, especially public words.
    1. Not _seasoned_ prophets (yet).

    2. Do unto others as you would have them do unto you...

    3. God does not establish His _credibility_ through _novices_. (We are still novices)

    4. If you enjoy strong corrective words you'd better _examine_ your _heart_.

        Psalm 37:21   *The righteous shows mercy.*

        Proverbs 10:12   *Love covers a multitude of sins.*

        Psalm 85:8-13   *I will hear what the Lord will speak for He will speak   peace.*

 Mercy and truth have met together.

Notice the order, first mercy , then truth.

5.   *John 1:17*   Make this your <u>foundation.</u>

                  Law = Old Testament   Grace = New Testament

                  Who are you speaking for?

6.   Correction through <u>wisdom</u> and <u>grace</u> brings <u>life</u> and <u>encouragement</u> .

      Litmus test: How do we correct our spouse or the person you are the most familiar with? This is the degree to which you should correct.

JESUS CHRIST: "*Don't ever beat my sheep, says the Lord.*"

E. Realize God has not brought us into a <u>judgment</u> dispensation.

PROPHETIC APPLICATION: Ministering as a Team

Recognize and submit to the Pastor/Leader. Prophets are sent to build and submit.

Show great respect. Be affirming. Be attentive to other's ministry. Never contradict, don't repeat words, if you received the same word, hold it.

Learn to handle the microphone. Don't ever interrupt someone ministering. Don't hog the show; let others flow as much or more than yourself.

No "I" in T.E.A.M.

Don't go too long. Don't preach your doctrine when prophesying. Better to be short than long. CONDENSE. It is too difficult for people in the congregation that are not being ministered to.

Lay hands-on people wisely, with respect. Call people out by color of clothing, not color of skin (i.e. my black brother, etc.).

PROTOCOL: "TIDBITS OF WISDOM"

1. God gives the Truth; the delivery is up to us.

2. Right revelation, Wrong interpretation, Wrong application.

3. Only say what God says, don't add to it and don't try to figure it out.

4. Let people make up their own minds, don't help them out.

5. Ask questions of the Lord, if He doesn't answer, ask the person.

6. Don't assume anything, ever!

7. Even if God shows you something about a church or pastor, don't share it. Only share it if the pastor asks then only if the Lord gives you permission.

8. First learn to be an intercessor and then a prophet. If not, you may end up like Balaam or Gehazi.

9. Playing to the grandstand or audience will always get you into trouble.

10. Remember prophet, you are only one word away from being a jackass.

11. Assumption is <u>always</u> deadly.

12. Don't listen to the unjust judge. (your mind)

13. Never uncover or expose. Don't be unethical.

14. Don't go <u>anywhere</u> God has not sent you.

15. Don't say <u>anything</u> God has not said to you.

16. Don't ever call people out by race.

17. Don't prophesy the eternal word!

18. Put the Word in the best package you can.

19. Don't expound, give what you get.

20. Don't counsel, prophesy.

21. Don't get hung up on eschatology or doctrine.

22. Learn to take a negative and make it a positive.

23. Use extreme caution in public.

24. Always, always, always seek to bless others regardless of the cost.

25. Never minister to anyone differently than you would the Lord Jesus.

26. Always walk worthy of the calling and don't be thin-skinned.

27. Remember you prophesy in part. Don't get puffed up, you're human.

28. Always be in the Word, always be with the Lord.

29. Always check your heart. Do I love God's people? (Never beat my sheep)
30. <u>Never Quit</u>!!!

LEVEL III PITFALLS

INTRODUCTION

A. God _always_ works first on our manhood, _maturity_, marriage, and _motive_ before He concentrates on our _ministry_.

Allow God to perfect your...

Morality, methods, motives, message, manners, money, ministerial ethics.

B. God must first _purge_ and _purify_ us before we can _affect_ the _multitudes_.

C. **1 Thessalonians 5: 23** "Now may the God of peace Himself sanctify you completely; may your whole spirit, soul, and body be preserved blameless at the coming of our Lord Jesus Christ."

Maturity = Accountability + Responsibility

We will look at several areas of caution and concern which could cause the prophetic minister to fall into the pit.

You are already in God's PIT.

_P_rophet – _I_n – _T_raining   _P. I. T._

D. The Word of God clearly teaches that the saints do not choose their member-ship ministry within the Body of Christ.

1. *1 Corinthians 12:18*

2. _Members_ do not _call_ themselves to a 5-fold ministry of their _choosing_ .

3. *Ephesians 4:8, 11* He gave some to be...

4. *1 Corinthians 12:28* God has set in the church apostles & prophets.

5. *John 15: 16* You did not choose Me, but I chose you and ordained you.

E. The gifts and _callings_ of God are based on His _sovereignty_, not on _human_ worth or _persistence_ in requesting a _position_.

   1. To whom much is _given_, much is _required._

   2. Jesus has a special love for those called to _represent_ Him. He has given to them of His own _nature_, grace, gifts, and _ministry._ So those to whom much is given, _much_ is _required._ James 3:1 declares that these will be judged more strictly.

   3. This principle of _accountability_ seems to apply _strongly_ to those called to be prophets.

   4. Those called to speak _directly_ for Him with "thus saith the Lord" are given _much._

   5. Much more is required of prophets in the areas of _obedience_, integrity, righteousness, and _Christ-likeness_.

      Dr. Bill Hamon has coined the phrase "Prophetic Pitfalls." These pits are satanic snares which, if not avoided, will cause a prophetic minister to be destroyed.

      This third level of training is designed to reveal the pitfalls of the devil and to activate your gifting to a new level of integrity and powerful accuracy. Power and purity in ministry to reach your predestined purpose; to be conformed into the image of Jesus Christ, the Great Prophet.

F. Weed Seeds, Root Problems and Character Flaws

   1. Weed seeds are _attitudes_ within a person's heart that will _spring_ into a dangerous weed of wrong _behavior._

   2. Problems _occur_ when weed seeds are _allowed_ to sprout, because they will _grow._

G. The _root_ system becomes _intertwined_ with the roots of the Word of God within your _heart_.

   1. Why are root problems dangerous?

In the natural, the roots of weeds rob nutrients that would normally be going into the fruit-bearing plants.

2. Realize that God does not _uproot_ tares until _after_ the harvest.

3. Winter _season,_ trees cannot be pruned while _fruit_ is on the branches.

4. God will _wait_ until your _winter_ season to _uproot_ your bad _roots._

H. However we can _uproot_ small weeds while they are still _attitudes_ and not yet _fully_ matured _plants._

1. _Deal_ with weed seeds _before_ they become _root_ problems.

2. Root _problems_ will become intertwined with _personality_ and _performance_ .

3. Quick _repentance_ is the _key_ for digging up weed seeds!

I. *Romans 11:22*

1. God's _goodness_ in _choosing_ us.

2. God's _severity_ in training and _maturing_ us.

3. Heaven in the _calling;_ Hell in the _perfecting._

4. Remember: There is no _limit_ in what God can and will do to _perfect_ us.

J. Do you still want to be a Prophet?

1. Root of bitterness - Hebrews 12:15

2. Root of evil - 1 Timothy 6:10

3. Holy Roots - Romans 11:16

NOTES

ELIJAH PITFALL 1 KINGS 17-19 (STUDY)

A. Elijah demonstrated many admirable qualities of a Prophet of God.

   1. Prayer

   2. Faith

   3. Obedience to the _voice_ of the Lord.

   4. _Willingness_ to put his life on the line.

   5. _Challenged_ the people of God.

B. Character _flaws_ existed in Elijah's life which would cause him to be susceptible to _satanic_ pitfalls.

   1. The _pity_ of _self-pity_ .

      a. Elijah's reaction to Jezebel's response to his destruction of the false prophets was a plunge from powerful prophetic ministry to a pit of self-pity and pessimism.

   2. Kings 19:4-8

      a. Prayers of self-pity: "God _kill_ me. I am the _only_ one left who _serves_ You."

      b. Elijah was _mighty_ in prophesying and _performance_ but weak in _personality_ , attitude, and _adjustment_ to _rejection_ and persecution.

      c. Elijah could not handle _rejection_ and _persecution_ .

      d. Prophets are sometimes placed in extreme situations with high stakes.

         (1) Success vs. Failure

         (2) Acceptance vs. Rejection

         (3) Vindication vs. Humiliation

         (4) Life vs. Death

      e. Many times _successes_ are followed by _rejection_ and _threats_ of destruction.

Avoid the pit of discouragement

Pit of discouragement

Disappointment

   Discouragement

      Bitterness

         Resentment

            Self-Pity

               Persecution Complex

                  Anger

                     Critical Spirit

                        Deception

                          Delusion

3. Once a critical spirit takes over, you become a law unto yourself, taking on a spirit of rejection and becoming unreachable through self-delusion.

    a. "Everybody is against me"

    b. "Nobody understands me"

    c. "Nobody appreciates me"

4. Cave mentality: "I am the only one left", opens you to a spirit of error.

FOUNDATIONS FOR
SPIRITUAL MATURITY

SELF EVALUATION

MANHOOD: God is more concerned with making men and women of God than He is with our commissioning.
- Does my character reflect Christ? YES/NO

MINISTRY: Make full proof of our ministry: properly ministering both; The *Word of God* and the *Spirit of God.*
- Is the word I speak positive, pure and proven? YES/NO

MESSAGE: Are you established in present Truth?
- Am I a studier of God's Word? YES/NO

MATURITY: Mature believers manifest the characteristics of agape love!
- Am I easily corrected? YES/NO

MARRIAGE: Our marriage should reflect the loving relationship between Christ and His bride the church.
- Is my spouse my best earthly friend? YES/NO

METHODS: Hypocrisy, one of the greatest underminers of ministry; Unchristian, ungodly methods destroy the testimony of Jesus!
- Do my actions line up with my words? YES/NO

MANNERS: Love is mannerly; Our manners must be on a higher plane than that of the world.
- Am I on time, or do I keep people waiting? YES/NO

MONEY: Areas of concern regarding money: Heart attitude, motives, Biblically ordered priorities.
- Do I have a desire for earthly things more than God's Kingdom? YES/NO

MORALITY: Honor God with your body; Sexual immorality has no place in the life of the Christian.
- Guys, are you fighting lust and perversion? YES/NO
- Ladies, are you fighting fantasies? YES/NO

MOTIVES: Motives always deal with the core of the man; HIS HEART!
- Do we minister in order to serve, or be seen? YES/NO

WE ARE ONLY AS STRONG AS OUR WEAKEST LINK!

INTRODUCTION Acts 6:1-5 7:51-8:1

A. 3 P's   Proper   Personal   Preparation

*   For *maturing* and *maintaining* ministry.

*   For *discerning* true and false ministers.

*   Personal *character* reflecting Christ-like *character* is the foundation for all ministry.

B.   **1 Corinthians 13:1-3** Says, "*Gifting* without Christ-like *character*, profits us nothing". Our works in the kingdom of God must be built on a solid base of *personal* purity and *maturity*.

When we fail to press into godly character we open ourselves up to the deception that we are *pleasing* God because *gifts* are still happening through our lives.

Romans 11:29 says, "... the gifts and *callings* of God are without repentance.

"Without change of mind" –God will still bless others regardless of your heart.

C.   **Matthew 7:13-23**

It is time for the church to walk in true *discernment*.

* Discerning *between* good and evil.

* Discerning between *fruits* and *gifts*, not running after every preacher who moves in the gifts of the Spirit. Paul said, "follow after me as I follow after Christ."

God desires our being conformed into the image of His Son more so than us looking good ministering the gifts.

MANHOOD

A. **Genesis 1:26-27** God created mankind in His _image_, according to his likeness then God gave man _dominion_ over the earth.

Note: First God made, then He commissioned. This principle has not changed. God is more concerned with making _men_ and _women_ of God than He is with our commissioning.

**EPHESIANS 1:17-18**

Wisdom _revelation_ in the _knowledge_ of Christ: THEN the eyes of your understanding will be enlightened to know what the hope of His calling is.

Many of us have the principle in reverse. We press toward the calling first rather than gaining the wisdom and revelation that comes through knowing Christ.

B. _**ROMANS 8:29**_ God predestined us to be _conformed_ to the image of Jesus Christ.

Conformed: render like, union with, completeness, resemblance, similar, jointly formed, fashioned like, adjustments to shape and likeness.

* Philippians 3:10   * James 5:10-11

Conforming process = suffering

Think of Adam before the fall, this is what God intended for man through eternity.

Suffering + Patience = _Conformation_

Romans 8:17 says, "...we are children, heirs of God, joint heirs with Christ if in fact we suffer with Him..."

Hebrews 2:10 declares, "Jesus was made perfect through suffering..."

We are to be made _perfect_ complete through _suffering_, allowing God's conforming process in our lives.

"If we are to be joint heirs with Christ, we must allow this process."

**Don't Be Deceived:** Performance is **NOT** a standard for evaluation!

Christ-like character must be our standard.

2 Corinthians 3:18 NASB – Transformed; Transfigured, Greek: "metomorphoo"

Paul did not boast in his _position_ as apostle or the signs and _wonders_ of his ministry. He boast in being _changed_ from glory to _glory._

Our highest calling and most _important_ goal is not to be great ministers, but to be like Christ, a servant to all.

We tend to grow the least when everything is going _smoothly_. Our years of preparation for mature _manhood_ and _womanhood_ are more important than our years of ministry.

Without proper personal preparation, our mighty ministry performances will become _perverted_ and cannot _permanently_ endure!

SERVANTS: In the natural, servants don't get waited on, they're not important, not in the limelight, they don't seek attention.

REMEMBER: Well done my good and faithful servant.
       Make Christ-like character our aim, our goal.

Our transformation into Christ like character is what God is primarily after, so whatever happens to us is working together for our good towards that goal. Remember there are no _good_ or _bad_ times in God's ultimate _purpose_.

2 CORINTHIANS 4:15-18   *ALL THINGS ARE FOR YOUR SAKE…*

As Christians we really don't have problems just predestined purposes ordained by God to conform us to the image of Christ Jesus.

C. Our physical bodies will be transformed from mortal to immortal.
 Philippians 3:21; 1 Corinthians 15:51; 1 Thessalonians 4:17

 However, Christ like character comes through a different transformation
 Romans 12:2   By the renewing of our minds.
 1 John 3:2-3   Everyone who has this hope purifies himself, just as He is pure.

MINISTRY

A. <u>Matthew 7:15-16</u> Jesus declared *false* prophets or false *ministers* would come as *wolves* in sheep's clothing, but that we could know the true from the false by their *fruits*.

Questions:

1. How long does the positive effect of our *ministry* last?

2. Is there *abiding* fruit?

3. After the excitement is over what *remains* that is of *value*?

4. Does our ministry *manifest* the *anointing* of God, or is there more *talk* than true *power*?

5. Is our preaching or ministry *productive*?

6. Is the *word* we speak *positive*, pure and *proven*?

7. Have we been *accurate*? Has our ministry *produced* the fruit of the Spirit in those to whom we have *ministered*?

8. Has our *preaching* or *prophesying* or *teaching* caused people to *stumble* or have we *discredited* the ministry in any way?

1 CORINTHIANS 2:4-5, 4:20   Power and Demonstration

My Preaching and message were not with wise and persuasive words, but with a ***demonstration of the Spirit and Power***, so your faith will not rest on man's words or wisdom, but on God's power.

The *Kingdom* of God depends not on talk, but on *power*!

As ministers of the New Testament, we have no *excuse* for not demonstrating the *supernatural* manifestation of *spiritual* gifts in our *ministry*!

WHY DO WE SETTLE FOR LESS?

1 Corinthians 6:3-10; No offense to ministry

We must always *evaluate* our ministry to see whether we have caused any to stumble.

2 Corinthians 12:10 We must _endure_ hardship, opposition, hard work, slander and sometimes deprivation, if we are willing to _endure_ we'll not give genuine cause to _condemn_ our work!

This is not to say that _criticism_ or controversy won't follow us Paul was saying "we should suffer for the sake of _truth_ and _righteousness_ in our ministry, not _reproach_ or shame we may bring.

Don't erect _unnecessary_ stumbling blocks that cause _undue_ offense!

B.   _**"Function in full Authority"**_   **2 Corinthians 3:4-6 NIV**

Vs. 5   Not that we are _sufficient_ of ourselves... But our sufficiency is in _God_.

Vs. 6   Who has made _us_ able, competent _ministers_ of the New Testament.

Vs. 5   Reveals _humility_

These go hand in hand!

Vs. 6   Reveals _confidence_

Paul refers to us as ministers of the New Testament, not ministers of the _letter_ but of the _Spirit_.

The letter without the _Spirit_ kills, the letter with the Spirit gives _life_.

We MUST have a balanced diet of the Word and the Spirit!

We must _study_ the Word! The Word of God is our _absolute_ standard.

New Testament ministers are those who release both _Word_ and _Spirit_.

Example: Jesus' death on the cross and resurrection from the grave are equally important. However, one does not take precedence over the other. We must not shy away from ministering the Spirit of God. Jesus gave us the example: first He brought the word then He moved in power.

Make full proof of our ministry: properly ministering both:

The Word of God and the Spirit of God!

MESSAGE

A. **2 Peter 1:12**   Though you know them…   verse. 1-11

Established in <u>present</u> truth.   "Present Manna"

<u>Ephesians 4:15</u>   Speak the truth in love.

Our message should be <u>life</u> giving <u>present</u> truth, presented in such a <u>fashion</u> that is thoroughly <u>scriptural</u>, doctrinally <u>sound</u>, a well- balanced diet with the <u>whole</u> counsel of the <u>word</u> of God.

Our message must be delivered in love!

Not only must the content of the message be accurate or right, so must the *<u>spirit</u>* of the *<u>message</u>*.

WE CAN BE DOCTRINALLY CORRECT & SPIRITUALLY WRONG!

Teaching, preaching and ministering theologically *<u>correct</u>*.

Spirit delivered (tone & motivation) vs. Spirit that is out of order.

Not directed by divine love…
        Example the Pharisees: right doctrine, wrong spirit.

Attitude and *<u>relationship</u>* with God is the *<u>key</u>*.

        Guard from: *<u>Pride</u>*, narrow-*<u>mindedness</u>* and *<u>self</u>*-righteousness.

Also, the *<u>opposite</u>* is true…
        Example: the Mormons

Right spirit, wrong <u>doctrines</u>.

Personality *<u>cannot</u>* be our *<u>judge</u>,* only the *<u>Bible</u>*.

Just because we see supernatural power doesn't prove *<u>biblical</u>* soundness.

In the last days more power will be released, we must judge by the Word.

False signs…   2 Timothy 4:2-5 NLB make full proof of the ministry...

B. **_MARK 16:20_** "God confirms His Word"

God does not confirm us; or our great statements of faith; nor our egos

GOD CONFIRMS HIS WORD

God is not concerned with His _reputation_.   Philippians 2:7

He made of Himself no _reputation_. Jesus did the will of God to _please_ the Father, not to be _popular_.

God confirms His Word! Not our flesh or desires or our presumption! God is not concerned with our PRIDE!

He does want us to have a good _report_ and for us to accomplish His _will_.

But our _popularity_ is not high on His list.

Revelation of this truth will release us from a great deal of pressure.

"No servant is greater than his Master" "I must decrease so He can increase."

God's Word has power in and of itself. He therefore _confirms_ that power through signs, not the Preacher _good_ or _bad_.

Romans 1:16

The gospel is the power of God unto salvation, not the one preaching it!

We should not be taken back at Judgment Day, when _many_ who did works are _sent_ away.

2 Timothy 2:15   _Study_ to show **YOURSELF** _approved_.

STUDY = APPROVAL = NOT ASHAMED = RIGHT DIVIDER

Is our message right on? Not watch dogs for God's Kingdom.

Remember: **Hebrews 6:1-3**   Let us go on to perfection…   Completion

Retain the basics and incorporate all presently restored biblical truth in our message.

MATURITY

A. *1 TIMOTHY 3:6*   Newly Planted: young converts "Greek"

The Bible warns us not to place *new* Christians in places of *leadership*; new believers must be *given* time to be *proven* and to *mature*.

Emotional, Social and Spiritual *maturity*.

Maturity does not automatically come with *time*.

(Traits of Christian Maturity)

Love		Godly wisdom	
Joy		Pure wisdom	
Peace		Consideration	
Patience		Submissive	
Kindness	Galatians	Merciful	James 3:17
Goodness	5:22-23	Impartial	
Faithfulness		Sincere	
Gentleness		Self-control	

Too many leaders have failed to allow the dealings of *God* and *hard* experiences (*tribulation* and *trials*) to cultivate in them divine *maturity*.

MATURE BELIEVERS MANIFEST THE CHARACTERISTICS OF AGAPE LOVE!

I CORINTHIANS 13:4-8

Patient	Not easily angered
Kind	No record of wrongs
Not envious	Not delighting in evil, rejoicing with the truth
Not boasting	Always protecting
Not proud	Trusting
Not rude, not self-serving	Never failing, hoping & persevering

Maturity Questionnaire

Am I Patient?   Am I Kind?

How do I behave?

Do I get upset when things are not my way?

Am I merciful?   Am I easily corrected?

Am I teachable?

Do I anger easily?

Am I trustworthy?

Immature people tend to be *unapproachable* untouchable, *defensive* and overly *sensitive*.

God not only expects *spiritual* growth, but *emotional* growth as well.

Selfishness, *possessiveness* and *desire* for attention can only be considered

childish and immature. Not fitting for *mature* sons and daughters of God.

I CORINTHIANS 13: 11   NIV

B. Scriptural, Doctrinal, Theological Maturity

Are we growing in our theology and understanding of scripture?

Ephesians 4:14 NLB   Are we still *infants*?

Hebrews 5: 12-14   Solid food for the *mature*.

Look to produce *fruits* of maturity first rather than *giftedness* only!

C. What is a mature person?

Mature people are those who have, and *continue* to, overcome character *flaws*.

We will never reach our potential unless *we* allow God to bring our *manhood* and *womanhood* to *maturity*.

The key to *victory*: Loving Jesus with our whole being and allowing *Him* to be Lord of *every area* of our *lives*.

* Philippians 2:12-15

"Work out your *own* salvation with fear and trembling. For it is *God* that works in *you* both to will and to *do* His good *pleasure*."

"Do all things without murmuring and disputing that ye may be blameless, the sons of God without rebuke in the midst of a crooked and perverse nation, among who you shine as lights in the world."

SALVATION: SOTERIA = GREEK ROOTS SOZO

Deliverance, health, salvation, perseverance, wholeness

MARRIAGE

A. <u>Ephesians 5: 22-23</u>   NRSV NLB

Our marriages should *reflect* the loving *relationship* between Christ and His bride the *church*.

HUSBANDS: Love your wives with Christ *kind* of love. Love your wife as you *love* yourself, be *joined* to your wife, *one* with *her*. Be *considerate* to your wife and *show* her *honor*.

WIVES: *Respect* and submit to your husbands as you *would* the *Lord*. Accept the *authority* of your husband. Walk in a gentle and *quiet* spirit, which is *precious* in the *sight* of the *Lord*.

BOTH: Have unity of *spirit*, sympathy, show *love* for one another, be *tenderhearted*, and have a humbleness of *mind*. Realizing that *both* are heirs *together* in the grace of *life*.

1 Peter 3:7   Declares, "if we walk this way our prayers will not be hindered."

Our *spouse* must be our best earthly friend.

NO MINISTRY MATES OR SPIRITUAL SPOUSES = EMOTIONAL ADULTERY

If someone is growing closer to us than our spouse, we are in danger of "Emotional Adultery."

B. **1 TIMOTHY 3:2-5** *NLB*

Our *homes* must be in *biblical* order.

Our *children* must be well *disciplined* and *submissive* and respectful.

HOWEVER: Our children are not called to be the perfect model for sake of the ministry.

Do not place *unrealistic* expectations on your children, this will lead them to *resent* and *rebel* against the church.

Don't expect your children to make _continual_ sacrifices for the sake of ministry.

GOD, WIFE, <u>children</u> (FAMILY), MINISTRY.

WE MUST HAVE OUR _priorities_ STRAIGHT.

(MINISTRY MUST NOT COMPETE WITH FAMILY)

At times we will have to draw the line between ministry to _others_ and ministry to our _family_.

> <u>**NOTE:**</u>   _"If we don't minister to our family we won't have a family. If we don't have a family, we won't have a ministry"._

> *   _IF WE CAN'T CARE FOR OUR OWN HOUSEHOLD, HOW CAN WE CARE FOR THE HOUSEHOLD OF GOD!_

METHODS

HYPOCRISY ONE OF THE GREATEST UNDERMINERS OF MINISTRY.

Hypocrisy: To hide under a false _appearance_. A _feigning_ to be what one is not, or to _believe_ what one does not, to act the _part_, not genuine. One who _affects_ virtues or _qualities_ he does not possess.

TITUS 1:16 NLB   They claim to _know_ God, but by their _actions_ they _deny_ Him.

*   _Hypocrisy simply put is when our actions don't line up with our words._

UNCHRISTIAN, UNGODLY METHODS DESTROY THE TESTIMONY OF JESUS.

Ghandi: "I would believe in your Jesus if it were not for you Christians."

* MINISTRY METHODS MUST BE RIGIDLY RIGHTEOUS *

No mercy on the _works_ of the _flesh_. In ministry, as with other _endeavors_ the _end_ does not _justify_ the _means_.

God does not need us to _exaggerate_ testimonies to make Him or His _power_ look good.

NO "EVANGELASTICALLY SPEAKING"   _ROMANS 3:7-8_   _NLB_

A LIE CANNOT SERVE THE TRUTH : NEVER...   NEVER !

(Rom 1:18 KJV) "For the wrath of God is revealed from heaven against all ungodliness and unrighteousness of men, who hold the truth in unrighteousness;"

No allowance for _manipulation_ and _deception_.

HONEST IN FINANCES

Practice _absolute_ honesty in _finances_. Total _integrity_ with all ministry _dealings_. Our ministry _methods_ must not _manipulate_ people to response. _Evil_ must not be used in any _Christian_ endeavor.

We have seen God's judgment on unethical ministry practices; the judgment will become more severe. We must circumcise our flesh before we can enter the land of promise.

DO OUR METHODS BRING REPROACH TO THE KINGDOM OF GOD?

HONESTY

INTEGRITY   **"FOUNDATION STONES FOR OUR METHODS"**
UPRIGHTNESS

We must not _hold_ the truth in _unrighteousness_!

Good end results don't _justify_ unscriptural _methods_!

MANNERS

TITUS 1:7-8 3:1-2   NRSV

Blameless	Hospitable
Not overbearing	Lover of good
Not quick tempered	Prudent
Not addicted to wine	Upright
Not violent	Holy
Not greedy for gain	Self-controlled
Obedient	Avoids disputes
Submissive to authority	Gentle
Prepared for every work	Considerate
Speaks evil of no man	Courteous

Our *manners* must be on a *higher plane* than that of the world.

Love must be the *rule* for Christian *leader's* relationships.

LOVE IS MANNERLY

EVEN IF OUR *ministry* IS CORRECT, *accurate* AND *scriptural*, IF OUR *manners* DON'T *reflect* CHRIST JESUS THEN WE *close* PEOPLE'S *spirits* TO RECEIVING THE *desired* EFFECT.

RUDE

CRUDE

ILL MANNERED   Ministers cannot portray Christ with these manners

OBNOXIOUS

COLOSSIANS 4:6 NLB

Let your *speech* always be *gracious* seasoned with *salt*, so that *you* may know how you *ought* to *answer* everyone.

Speak evil of no one.   No *slander*, no *backbiting*, no *murmuring*.

Psalm 141:3   Set a guard over my mouth O Lord. Keep watch over the doors of my lips.

James 1:19   Let _everyone_ be quick to _listen_, slow to _speak_, slow to _anger_. For your anger does not _produce_ God's _righteousness_.

JAMES 3: 1-18   **NLB**

If any think that they are _religious_ and do not bridle their tongues, but _deceive_ their hearts, their _religion_ is _worthless_.

NO FOUL LANGUAGE OR COURSE LANGUAGE

"NO BARNYARD TERMINOLOGY"

EPHESIANS 4:29-30 NLB

Do not let any _unwholesome_ talk come out of your mouths. Only what is _helpful_ in our _vocabulary_. Living and _speaking_ cannot be _separated_, they go _hand_ in _hand_.

Swearing is a _weak_ mind trying to be _forceful_.

Matthew 12:34   **Out of the abundance of the heart ...**

It is simple, if foulness comes out, ask the Lord to deliver you from it and place a guard over your lips.

*   Bad _manners_ will _discredit_ our ministries!

QUESTIONNAIRE

1. Are we on *time* or do we keep people *waiting*?

2. Do we show *gratitude* for acts of kindness?

3. Are we *polite* and *thankful* to those serving us?

4. Are we *impatient* and *demanding*?

5. Do we *wait* our turn to *speak* or do we *interrupt*, feeling like our *point* is more *important*.

MINISTERS OF GOD ARE CALLED TO BE LADIES AND GENTLEMEN

MONEY

Money is neither good nor evil in and of itself!

Money is an *inanimate* object with neither *virtue* or *vice*.

Money is simply the *medium* of exchange for earthly *things*.

Money is earth's *currency* for purchasing *goods* and *services*.

1 TIMOTHY 6:10   **Why do many of us desire to be rich?**

Wrong perspectives!

The love of money is the root of all evil, and in their eagerness to be rich some have wandered away from the faith and pierced themselves with many pains and sorrows.

The Bible has never taught that it is wrong to be wealthy.

Deuteronomy 8:18 Says, "it is the Lord that *gives* thee the *power*

to *obtain* wealth that *He* might *establish* His *covenant*.

3 John 2   Declares it is God's will for His people to prosper and be in good health, even as their souls prosper.

WE ARE NOT TO HAVE A LOVE FOR EARTHLY THINGS   *(1JOHN 2:15-17)*

Matthew 6:33

Seek ye first The Kingdom Of God...

Seeking the Kingdom of God and His *righteousness* first is not an *easy* task; it cannot be *accomplished* with *conflicts* of *interest*. If we truly seek *after* God *first* with all our heart, our *other* God inspired endeavors will be *fruitful* and will be *accomplished* in peace.

Christians can have money, but money cannot have Christians!

AREAS OF CONCERN REGARDING MONEY

1. Heart Attitude

2. Motives

3. Biblically ordered priorities

Wealth can be used to fulfill the love for earthly power, which is resident in the sinful nature. Money, which in and of itself is not sinful, can be used to fulfill sinful desires.

Such as: Lust of the flesh
                     Lust of the eyes
                     Pride of Life

On the other hand, money can be used as a *tool* to *fulfill* divinely *inspired* purposes.

1 Timothy 6:3-11   NLT

Verse 5—Robbed of the *truth*.

Think *godliness* is a *means* of financial *gain*.

Verse 6—*Godliness* with *contentment* = great gain.

Verse 9—Desires for *riches* = *destruction*.

Verse 11—Man of God *flee* from all this.

Temptations, Snares, and Heartaches are side effects of great wealth apart from God's will.

Parable of the Rich Man trying to get to heaven...

Climbing the High Mountain of "Financial Success"

Higher At the Top:

A. Less Vegetation...

B.   Faster and Harder winds

C.   Loneliness

COVETING = I WISH THIS, OR THAT

Covetousness   Winning the lotto, etc.

LUKE 12:15   **NO GREED ALLOWED!**

Watch out! Be on your guard against *all kinds of greed*, a man's life does not consist in the abundance of his possessions.

We, as *Men* and *Women* of God, must *reject* the *world's* view of success, i.e. the piling up of *great* wealth.

MATTHEW 6:24   *"CANNOT SERVE GOD AND MAMMON"*

QUESTION:

If God possesses all the wealth, (the earth is the Lord's and all that is therein) why then are we proud and arrogant, and desirous for more gain?

HEART ISSUE!

MORALITY

EPHESIANS 5:3   *COLOSSIANS 3:5*

It should go without saying that sexual immorality has no place in the life of the Christian especially the ministers. However, this is just not the case!

"HONOR GOD WITH YOUR BODY" 1 CORINTHIANS 6:9-10   18-20

Sexual Immorality Includes:

FANTASIES

MASTURBATION

PORNOGRAPHY

SEXUALLY AROUSING FILMS OR TELEVISION PROGRAMS

AREAS WHICH WILL LEAD US INTO TEMPTATION

MATTHEW 5:27-30   (HEART ATTITUDES IS WHAT WE ARE DEALING WITH)

QUESTIONS:

1. Is our *heart* right with *God* and *man*?
2. *What* is coming *out* of our *hearts*?
3. *Guys*, are you fighting *lust* and *perversion*?
4. *Ladies*, are you battling *fantasies*?
5. Wrong *thoughts* to *do*, but no *opportunity* to *act*.

It is not a sin to be tempted with a lustful thought.

Sin *occurs* when we fail to reject the *thought* and begin to *entertain* and

meditate upon the *sinful* suggestion with *desire* and enjoyment.

These are weed seeds in our heart and if not rejected will sprout to full grown, mature plants.

SEEDS = THOUGHTS   *PLANTS = ACTS*

1 TIMOTHY 5:2   Guidelines

The Apostle Paul gives us good guidelines:

Treat older women as <u>Mothers</u>.

With Absolute Purity

Treat younger women as <u>Sisters</u>.

The same   Older Men   Fathers

          Younger Men   Brothers

We wouldn't think of evil desires with our own mothers or sisters! Walk this way!

<u>**Matthew 13:24-30**</u>   **Parable of the Weed-Seeds**

"Every Thought Captive"

<u>*2 Corinthians 10:3-6*</u>   *(NRSV)*

Bring every <u>*thought*</u> and <u>*imagination*</u> of the <u>*mind*</u> into <u>*captivity*</u> to the <u>*mind*</u> of <u>*Christ*</u>.

Holy, virtuous biblical principles, practices, and thoughts!

<u>*PHILIPPIANS 4:8-9*</u>   *(NLT)*

Use the <u>*offensive*</u> weapon of the <u>*Word*</u> of <u>*God*</u>, the <u>*Sword*</u> of the <u>*Spirit*</u>.

<u>*2 TIMOTHY2:22*</u>   "Flee from youthful lust"

<u>*1 THESSALONIANS 5:22*</u>   "Abstain from all appearances of evil"

God deliver us from our <u>*heritage*</u>!

<u>***REMEMBER THE FLESH IS NEVER SATISFIED, NEVER, NEVER, NEVER!***</u>

MOTIVES   *PROVERBS 20:27*

ARE OUR MOTIVES FOR MINISTRY PURE?

ARE OUR MOTIVES FOR MINISTRY BECOMING PURE?

Does *fame* and *personal* glory need to be *dealt* with?

EXAMPLES: "NAME IN LIGHTS"

"KNOWN BY THOSE ON STAFF"

"NOTICED BY THOSE IN LEADERSHIP"

"NOTICED BY THE GUEST MINISTER"

"PRAYER RECEIVED BY ONLY THE PASTOR"

Motives always deal with the core of the man, his heart!

JEREMIAH 17:9-10   The *heart* is *deceitful* above all *things*, and *desperately* wicked, *who* can *know* it.

The *Lord* searches the *heart* and tries the *reins*.

We must not be deceived by the wickedness of our hearts. We won't if we will allow the Lord to search out our hearts.

PSALM 64:6   *"the heart is deep"*

PSALM 44:21   *"God knows the secret of the heart"*

PSALM 139:23   *"Search me O God and know my heart, try me and my thoughts, see if there be any wicked way in me and lead me in the way everlasting"*

THE HIDDEN MOTIVES OF THE MAN MUST BE RECOGNIZED AND PURIFIED.

*   We won't be _judged_ just for our _actions_, but for our _deeds_.

MOTIVES + ACTIONS = DEEDS

Matthew 6:1-8 (NLT)   "Be careful not to do your **acts of righteousness** before men, to be seen by them! No reward from your Father in Heaven"

1 Samuel 16: 7 (NLT) "Man looks at the outward appearance, but God looks on the intent of the heart"

HEBREWS 4: 12

A.   The Word will _divide_ soul and _spirit_.

B.   _Joints_ and _marrow_.

C.   _Discerner_ of the _thoughts_ and _intents_ of the _heart_.

"The heart has thoughts and intentions; these together form motives"

BEWARE OF THE WEAK LINK!

THE CHAIN IS ONLY AS STRONG AS ITS WEAKEST LINK. OUR MINISTRY IS ONLY AS STRONG AS OUR WEAKEST "M."

ASK THE LORD TO ANSWER THESE QUESTIONS FOR YOU:

1.   Do we minister in order to serve or in order to be seen?

2.   Are we addicted to the ministry (1COR16:15) of the saints or do we want to be recognized as great ministers?

3.   Are we motivated by a desire to fulfill God's will or by some personal drive (such as lust for power, fame pleasure, and wealth)?

4.   Do we minister out of a heart full of God's love?   If not, we will minister in vain

(1COR 13:2-3)

DON'T GET INTO CONDEMNATION!

GET CONVICTED, GET ADJUSTED, SO GOD CAN FULFILL HIS PLANS THROUGH YOUR LIFE!

WE ALL HAVE ROOM FOR <u>GROWTH, IMPROVEMENT, AND CORRECTION.</u>

<u>ALWAYS ALLOW OTHERS TO EVALUATE OUR TEN "M's."</u>

<u>CHARACTER IS FAR MORE IMPORTANT THAN GIFTING</u>!

DON'T BE DECEIVED, A DONKEY CAN GIVE THE WORD OF THE LORD, BUT ONLY YOU CAN BE TRANSFORMED INTO CHRIST'S IMAGE.

DON'T BE PROUD OF THE AREAS YOU FUNCTION IN WELL AND IGNORE THE AREAS THAT NEED ATTENTION AND ADJUSTMENT.

STRENGTHENING YOUR TEN "M's" IS THE BEST WAY TO MAINTAIN AND MATURE A GODLY CHARACTER THAT WILL PROVIDE YOUR MINISTRY WITH A SOLID FOUNDATION FOR GROWTH AND SUCCESS.

"RUN THE RACE, FINISH THE COURSE"

NOTES

NOTES

NOTES

THE FOUR KEY DIMENSIONS
OF PERSONAL PROPHECY

Every personal prophecy contains four key dimensions. Understanding what they are and how they work can help us better align our faith and actions with prophetic words we receive. This in turn will help our prophecies come to pass without the delays often attributed to a lack of knowledge and revelation. Here we describe the anatomy of personal prophecy through the mix of four essential and active spiritual ingredients:

9. The word of knowledge,
10. The word of wisdom,
11. Promises and
12. Conditions.

The section on the following pages provides definitions of these four areas in the context of prophecy interpretation along with a framework for their life application.

Once a prophecy has been ***transcribed***, it's helpful to highlight words, phrases or sentences matching the criteria under each dimension. Using different colors to highlight is one quick and easy way to do this. For example, you can

Use <u>red</u> for words of knowledge, <u>blue</u> for words of wisdom, <u>**purple**</u> for promises and **black** for conditions. Color-coding will make visual referencing much easier later on. As you prayerfully read through the prophetic word, pay close attention to what the Holy Spirit illuminates; what He causes to stand out the most to you. It should be noted that in some cases particular points may fall into more than one category. For instance, a word of wisdom may also relate to a condition.

Now it's time to take a look at the chart. After studying it prayerfully, begin practicing the important truths presented about the make-up of personal prophecy and how to cooperate with God to see them through to fulfillment. You'll be advancing God's will here on earth by better understanding and doing what He wants to accomplish in and through your life.

As God releases prophecies to each of us, they testify of who Jesus is- in all of His matchless power and glory (Rev. 19:10c). They reveal Him as our covenant-keeping, promise fulfilling Savior. And as He brings His written and spoken word to pass in our lives, we store up personal testimony after testimony to overcome the enemy's attempts to discredit God's faithfulness toward us (Rev. 12:11). Praise God!

Definitions & Applications

Identifying the Gifts of the Holy Spirit

1 Corinthians 12:4-11, Romans 15:14

Word of Knowledge

This serves as a true *faith builder* for the person receiving the prophetic word as precise details about their life are revealed through someone that doesn't have prior knowledge about them.

From the Strong's Concordance: G1108 gnosis, gno'-sis From G1097; knowing (the act), by implication) knowledge: - knowledge, science.

Definition:

- Supernatural revelation given by the Holy Spirit to a believer about specific facts in the mind of God for another. These facts are accurate and may give information about a person's past, present, or future.

- It is an instant knowledge from the Lord that the recipient has no way of knowing except that God reveals it.

Application: Make a list of every word of knowledge (Underlining in red) and praise God for them. Thank the Lord for speaking directly to you through the word of knowledge.

Word of Wisdom

This serves as a *direction giver*; this gift of the Spirit communicates such things like what to do, where to do it and when to do it.

From the Strong's Concordance: G4678 sophia, sof-ee'-ah From G46680; wisdom (higher or lower, worldly or spiritual): - wisdom.

Definition:

- The right use or the exercise of knowledge.

- Supernatural ability given by the Holy Spirit to impart special and specific insight, instruction, guidance, or counsel. It brings life-changing illumination and course-changing decisions when heeded.

Application: Take note of each word of wisdom. (<u>Underlining in blue</u>) Respond ***in faith*** by taking action with the direction given by the word of wisdom.

Promises

Each promise is a ***future revealer***. By them our future reality is plainly declared and decreed by God. Promises are at the very heart of prophecy, for they reveal the deep intentions of the Father's heart for us. They also create an incentive for us to trust and follow Him.

From the Strong's Concordance: <u>G1860</u> epaggelia, ep-ang-el-ee'-ah From <u>G1861</u>; an announcement (for information, assent or pledge; especially a divine assurance of good); - message, promise.

Definition:

- In Scripture, the promise of God is the declaration or assurance, which God has given in His Word of bestowing blessings on His people. Such assurance resting on the perfect justice, power, benevolence and immutable veracity of God, cannot fail of performance. *The Lord is not slack concerning His promises.* ***2 Peter 3***

- ***2 Pet. 1:3-4*** *NKJV...His divine power has given to us all things that pertain to life and godliness, through the knowledge of Him who called us by glory and virtue, by which have been given to us exceedingly great and precious promises, that through these you may be partakers of the divine nature...*

Application: Wage war in prayer for all promises identified. (**<u>Underlining in purple</u>**) Seek out, pray and appropriate the "divine precedence" of relatable Bible promises.

Conditions

Functioning as an ***obedience promoter***, a condition is a specific, clearly stated must-do requirement. Collectively they make up God's unique action agenda for us to follow.

Definition of Condition: To make terms; to stipulate.

Application: Any stipulation given by God in prophecy calls for deliberate and immediate action. (**<u>Underlining in black</u>**) Be careful to record and respond to the stipulations identified!

RECEIVING PROPHETIC MINISTRY
1 Corinthians 14:1-6

1. Have the Right Attitude

- **Desire:** Pursue love, and **<u>desire</u>** spiritual gifts….. **1 Corinthians. 14:1**

- **Covet:** Therefore, brethren **<u>covet</u>** earnestly to prophecy. **1 Corinthians 14:39** [KJV]

- **Faith:** So, then **<u>faith</u>** comes by hearing, and hearing by the Word of God. **Romans 10:17**

- **<u>Obedience</u>:** Be ye *doers* of the Word, and not hearers only, deceiving yourselves. **James 1:22**

- **Patience:** Imitate those who through faith and **<u>patience</u>** inherit the promise. **Hebrews 6:12[b]**

- **<u>Humility</u>:** The *humble* shall hear of it and be glad. **Psalm 34:2[b]**

- **Meekness**: Receive with **<u>meekness</u>** the implanted Word, which is able to save your souls. **James 1:21[b]**

- **Submission:** Obey those who rule over you, and be *submissive,* for they watch out for your souls, as those who must give an account. Let them do so with joy and not with grief, for that would be unprofitable for you. **Hebrews 13:17**

2. Record and Meditate

- **<u>Transcribe:</u>** "Write the vision and make it plain on tablets, that he may run who reads it. **Habakkuk 2:2**

- **<u>Do not neglect</u>** the gift that is in you, which was given to you by prophecy with the laying on of the hands of the eldership. Meditate on these things; give yourself entirely to them, that your progress may be evident to all. **1 Timothy 4:14-15**

- "Thus speaks the Lord God of Israel, saying: '**<u>Write in a book for yourself</u>** all the words that I have spoken to you. **Jeremiah 30:2**

3. Witness to Your Prophecy

- **<u>Acknowledge the Lord</u>:** Trust in the Lord with all your heart and lean not on your own understanding; In all your ways acknowledge Him, and He shall direct your paths. **Proverbs 3:5-6**

- **<u>Prove</u>:** Test all things; hold fast what is good.   **1 Thessalonians 5:21**

- **<u>Witness</u>:** – The Spirit Himself bears witness with our spirit that we are children of God. **Romans 8:16**

4. War a Good Warfare

- **Use prophecy as a sword:** For the weapons of our warfare are not carnal but mighty in God for pulling down strongholds. **2 Corinthians 10:4**

- **Speak the word:** This charge I commit to you, son Timothy, according to the prophecies previously made concerning you, that by them you may wage the good warfare. **1 Timothy 1:18**

5. Do Nothing Different Unless Clearly Directed to Do So

- Act on specifics through prayer and counsel (Pastoral Oversight). In the multitude of counselors there is safety. Don't run off halfcocked. Don't print business cards.

6. Understand God's Principles for Fulfillment

Mark 11:24 "*Therefore I say to you, whatever things you **ask** when you **pray believe** that you **receive** them, and you will **have** them.*

Hebrews 11:6 But without faith it is impossible to please Him, for he who comes to God must believe that He is, and that He is a rewarder of those who diligently seek Him.

2 Peter 1:1-4 Simon Peter, a bondservant and apostle of Jesus Christ, To those who have obtained like precious faith with us by the righteousness of our God and Savior Jesus Christ: Grace and peace be multiplied to you in the knowledge of God and of Jesus our Lord, as His divine power has given to us all things that pertain to life and godliness, through the knowledge of Him who called us by glory and virtue, by which have been given to us exceedingly great and precious promises that through these you may be partakers of the divine nature, having escaped the corruption that is in the world through lust.

NOTES

NOTES

NOTES

NOTES

NOTES

ABOUT THE AUTHOR

This book is dedicated to the legacy of Kenneth Peters Jr.
Ken gave his life to bring a present-day reformation to the body of Christ!

Ken went on to glory to his heavenly home on August 14, 2021.

Ken and Tonja Peters

Ken Peters was the founding apostle over a network of churches that are called by the Lord to be part of a transformational movement to restore the New Testament model/pattern of the Church.

At an early age the Lord began to give Ken prophetic visions with tremendous clarity and accuracy. In 1982, Ken accepted the call of God and began to move in the prophetic anointing. Ken served the Lord in ministry for over 35 years in various capacities, serving seven congregations. After many fruitful years in pastoral ministry, Ken and his wife, Tonja, began traveling full-time nationally and internationally as prophets, ministering the Word of the Lord to pastors, churches, and governmental leaders.

In 1999, Ken and Tonja founded Elijah/Prophetic Trumpet Ministries, an international ministry commissioned to build the Kingdom of God and bless churches abroad. In 2007, Ken and Tonja Peters founded and pastored The Gathering @ Corona, an Apostolic/Prophetic Reformation church. They assisted in planting and covering many Gathering churches throughout California and the United States and enjoyed leadership development, which eventually led to the establishing of The Gathering Network of Churches.

God placed a burning desire in Ken to see biblical apostolic/prophetic ministry restored and released throughout the entire body of Christ and to see apostolic government restored to the local church, the restoration of functioning five-fold ministers, training, equipping, and releasing the saints in their God given gifts to accomplish the work of ministry. Soon we will see the fullness of the body of Christ having freedom to cross-pollinate with the many streams of the manifestation of the Holy Spirit in the earth.

Made in United States
Cleveland, OH
29 December 2024

12784681R00044